NATIVE NATIONS OF THE

ARCTIC AND SUBARCTIC

BY MARIE POWELL

The Child's World®

Published by The Child's World®
1980 Lookout Drive • Mankato, MN 56003-1705
800-599-READ • www.childsworld.com

Acknowledgments
The Child's World®: Mary Berendes, Publishing Director
Red Line Editorial: Editorial direction and production
The Design Lab: Design
Content Consultant: Robert P. Wheelersburg, PhD,
Professor of Anthropology, Elizabethtown College,
NSF-Fulbright Arctic Scholar, University of Iceland

Photographs ©: Hinrich Baesemann/Picture-Alliance/DPA/AP
Images, cover, 2; Daderot CC 2.0, 1, 20; Tonya Hennessey CC
2.0, 3 (top), 9; Shutterstock Images, 3 (middle top), 12; James
Brooks CC 2.0, 3 (middle bottom), 15; Adam DuBrowa/Federal
Emergency Management Agency, 3 (bottom), 22, 23, 24; Galyna
Andrushko/Shutterstock Images, 5, 39; Pat and Rosemarie
Keough/Corbis, 6; Ton Koene/Visuals Unlimited/Corbis, 10;
Library of Congress, 11; Doug Ogden/Design Pics/Corbis, 14;
Werner Forman/Werner Forman/Corbis, 16; Natalie Fobes/
Corbis, 18; V. B. Scheffer/Library of Congress, 19; Peter Power/
ZumaPress/Corbis, 26, 27; Christopher J. Morris/Corbis, 29; F.
Lukasseck/Masterfile/Corbis, 30; Shin Okamoto/Shutterstock
Images, 31; Marilyn Angel Wynn/Nativestock Pictures/Corbis,
33; Lowell Georgia/Corbis, 34; John MacDougall/AFP/Getty
Images, 36

ISBN: 9781634070300
LCCN: 2014959801
Printed in the United States of America
Mankato, MN
July, 2015
PA02269

ABOUT THE AUTHOR

Marie Powell has written more than 30 children's books. She is also the author of the young adult fantasy novel *Hawk*. She lives in Regina, Saskatchewan.

An Inuit woman wears a traditional jacket with a hood made from wolf fur.

TABLE OF CONTENTS

ARCTIC

OCEAN

GREENLAND

Gulf of
Alaska

PACIFIC

OCEAN

CANADA

Hudson
Bay

UNITED STATES

ATLANTIC

OCEAN

MEXICO

Gulf of
Mexico

KEY

ARCTIC
NATIVE NATIONS

SUBARCTIC
NATIVE NATIONS

N
W E
S

CHAPTER ONE

ARCTIC AND SUBARCTIC NATIVE NATIONS

The northern part of North America is one of the coldest places in the world. But more than 20 Native Nations call it home. The land covers most of Alaska and northern Canada. It includes mountains, the icy coast along the Arctic Ocean,

The Alaskan tundra features grasses and shrubs but few trees.

Two Inuit women wear traditional clothing. Their parkas' designs are similar to the patterns on the rock wall.

and the barren **tundra** sometimes called the "frozen desert." From September to May, snow blankets the land. Temperatures reach -40 degrees Fahrenheit (-40°C) or as low as -80 degrees Fahrenheit (-62°C) with the windchill.

Countless generations of people survived the cold environment by fishing and by hunting caribou, whales, and seals. To keep dry, they wore sealskins as boots and leggings. For warmth, they wore caribou **hides** as jackets. Today, this traditional clothing is used mostly during ceremonies and special occasions. For everyday use, people wear jeans, T-shirts, and other modern clothes. Hunting and fishing are still important for the economy, but Native Peoples now use motorboats, snowmobiles, or all-terrain vehicles. They live in houses heated by modern means such as electricity. Although members of the numerous Native groups are citizens of Canada and the United States, most Native Nations are self-governing. They have their own leaders and make their own laws. Some people live on land set aside by the national government. Others live on their own land or in cities.

The Arctic region stretches across the northernmost part of North America, along 5,000 miles (8,000 km) of coastline. It borders the Pacific Ocean, the Arctic Ocean, the Atlantic Ocean, and the Arctic Circle. The main nations that call the Arctic home are the Inuit, the Yup'ik, and the Unangan. Most Arctic people live in small villages near the coast during the winter months. They hunt seals on the ice and whales in open water. In the summer they switch to a

nomadic lifestyle. They move to small camps along inland rivers where they fish and hunt caribou.

The Subarctic region includes much of Alaska and Canada. The Subarctic is farther south than the Arctic, but temperatures on winter days are often still below freezing.

This region is mainly tundra. It also has evergreen forests with berries and other plants for food. Researchers often divide the many nations living there into two language groups. Athabaskan is spoken in the west, and Algonquian is spoken in the east. Most Algonquian speakers are part of the Cree, Ojibwe, and Innu nations.

Historically, people in the Arctic and Subarctic built their houses from a variety of natural raw materials. Snow houses, also called igloos, could be built quickly as temporary shelters for hunters. Larger, more permanent snow houses might have sleeping platforms of ice blocks covered with furs. Permanent houses were dug partly underground, supported by whale ribs and driftwood. People also lived in sod houses, round wigwams, birch-bark lodges, or animal-hide tents. Today, houses may be built on extra supports so they do not sink in mud during the spring.

A member of the Dene Nation speaks at a political event.

CHAPTER TWO

INUIT

The Inuit people live in northern Canada and Alaska, as well as Greenland and Siberia. They speak Inuktitut or Inupiat. In Canada, the Inuit are one of three recognized **aboriginal** peoples, along with the First Nations and the Métis. Half

A boy wears sun goggles to protect his eyes from the bright snow.

of Canada's 50,000 Inuit people live in Nunavut, a federal territory that was created in 1999. Nunavut has its own legislature and government. It is an example of growing political movements in the Arctic for **self-determination** of Native Peoples.

Historically, the Inuit were expert hunters of caribou and sea mammals. In the summer, they relied on caribou. This meat would be dried, smoked, or salted for winter. During winter they used **harpoons**, or barbed spears, to hunt seals through holes in the ice. They also ice-fished. Many Inuit children still play games related to hunting, which teach boys the skills necessary to obtain food.

The Inuit once used only **kayaks** or light boats made from animal hides when hunting on water. For transporting people and supplies, they used larger boats called *umiaks*.

An Inuit woman poses for a photograph in the early 1900s.

They also used sleds called *qamutiks*, which were pulled by dogs. Today a few people still use these traditional methods. Many more use motorboats, snowmobiles, and all-terrain vehicles.

An inukshuk stands on a mountain in British Columbia, Canada.

Hunting sea mammals often produced an abundance of food. This gave the Inuit time each year to concentrate on ceremonial activities such as singing and dancing. Drums are the basis of Inuit music and dancing. Inuit drums are made from hoops covered with caribou skin or walrus stomachs. Inuit women practice "throat singing" while facing each other. One woman begins by inhaling and exhaling in a short rhythm or pattern. The other follows with her pattern. They continue until one woman laughs or stops singing. They might use words or syllables. Or they might mimic wildlife or sounds from daily living.

Inuit artwork often involves carvings of animals or people. These carvings can be made of stone, bone, or ivory. By balancing rocks, the Inuit also create outdoor landmarks known as *inukshuks*. An *inukshuk* might be used to show directions, mark a path, or as a memorial. Sometimes the rocks are stacked in the shape of a person.

Clothing that keeps people warm and dry has always been a key factor in surviving the Arctic cold. For warmth on land, traditional Inuit clothing was made of animal skin and furs. Intestines or skin from sea mammals made some clothes waterproof. Men and women often wore similar clothing in layers to create warmth. Women's parkas included a large hood or pouch for carrying babies. Women most often made the clothing, usually by chewing the animal skins to make them soft. They sewed everything together tightly with thread made from animal tissue. Even the boots had layers. There was a stocking inside, a waterproof sealskin in the middle, and a fur slipper outside. The Inuit also made sun goggles from bone or wood. They cut slits into the goggles to protect their eyes from snow blindness.

SAY IT			
	sled	quamutik	(caw-moo-tick)
	thank you	qujannamiik	(coo-ya-na-mee-ick)
	polar bear	nanuq	(naa-nook)

CHAPTER THREE

YUP'IK

A Yup'ik woman prepares fish by a riverside in Alaska.

The Yup'ik people live in Alaska, northern Canada, and northeastern Russia. Today there are about 25,000 Yup'ik people. They are the largest Native group in Alaska.

Yup'ik dancers from Mount Edgecumbe High School take part in a parade.

Traditional Yup'ik people moved with the seasons from winter villages to summer camps. They settled near rivers and along the coast, following animal **migrations**. They often hunted seals and walruses. Sometimes they hunted inland animals such as caribou, bears, birds, and fish. Today many Yup'ik hunt and fish using modern boats and

15

A Yup'ik mask features a moon face.

snowmobiles. In many Yup'ik villages, people hunt and fish to add to their family diet.

An important part of the Yup'ik culture involves late-winter ceremonies with drumming, dancing, and storytelling. **Shamans** wear masks to connect to the spirit world to help heal sick people. These masks and ceremonies were banned after European contact in the 1800s because Christian missionaries believed them to be devil worship. Today, Yup'ik people use masks during special ceremonies to celebrate their traditional culture.

Many Native Nations are identified by the languages they speak. The main language group in the Arctic has two branches. One of these branches is the Yup'ik language. Today, about 10,000 people speak the Yup'ik language. The word *Yup'ik* translates as "the real people."

Yup'ik ceremonies involve several styles of dancing. Each style has specific rhythms and gestures. Dancing is combined with storytelling, songs, drumming, and masks. These masks are made to show animals and spirits as a main part of the ceremony. Some masks have teeth. Some are decorated with feathers and spots of colored paint. The meanings behind these masks are often personal to the one who creates the mask. Today, many of these masks can be seen in museums and collections.

CHAPTER FOUR

UNANGAN

The Unangan people believe in the living nature of water. Their villages in south and southwest Alaska are set up along coasts and waterways. Many live in the Aleutian Islands, which stretch for more than 1,100 miles (1,800 km) off the Alaska Peninsula.

An Unangan fisherman pulls his catch into the boat.

A group of Unangan children stand in front of a building in the 1930s.

Historically, the Unangan people had a more complex political system than the Inuit or Yup'ik. The village chief made decisions, and some members of the community ranked higher than others. Even their wooden hunting hats had meaning. Inexperienced hunters wore short visors. Those with more experience wore longer visors. Important

An Unangan hunting hat is decorated with elaborate patterns.

men wore the longest visors. The number of sea lion whiskers on a person's hat indicated the hunter's success.

Their first nonnative contact was with the Russians in 1741. The Russians referred to the Unangan as the Aleut. The Russians claimed the Unangan land and forced many Native Peoples to relocate. There were about 15,000 Unangan at the time. However, this number dropped drastically. This happened in part because of disease brought by nonnatives. It was also due to nonnative overhunting of the sea mammals that the Unangan needed for survival.

Today, Unangan children learn about their history through summer camps and school courses. Many families continue to fish and carry out seal hunts. About 3,600 are members of the Aleut Corporation. In a 1971 settlement, this corporation received $19.5 million and about 70,000 acres of land. The corporation funds a cultural foundation and provides scholarships.

The Museum of the Aleutians, located in Unalaska, has 500,000 objects. These include

Today the Unangan carry on traditions and ceremonies that began long before contact with nonnatives. After fall harvesting and berry gathering, traditional festivals and ceremonies begin. They involve masks, ceremonial dress, skin drums, bird-beak rattles, and whistles. Ceremonies continue throughout the winter in large communal houses called *qasgiqs*. Some ceremonies are spiritual, and some mark social occasions such as weddings and funerals. In 2007, archeologists found a 3,000-year-old whalebone mask. This showed that the Unangan have been performing their funeral ceremonies in a similar way for thousands of years.

Unangan artifacts dating back 9,000 years. It also shows contemporary pieces from Native artists.

NORTHERN ATHABASKAN

Northern Athabaskans perform a traditional dance.

The Northern Athabaskans, also known as the Dene Nation, live across 3,000 miles (4,800 km) in central Alaska and northwestern Canada. But Northern Athabaskans

Northern Athabaskan girls take part in a potlatch ceremony.

are not a single group. They include many different bands that speak more than 20 dialects.

There are about 12,000 Northern Athabaskans in Alaska alone. In Canada, they are one of the self-governing nations. The

Tribal Chief Jessica Boyle, left, speaks to a federal officer about recovery efforts after flooding occurred in the community.

groups include the Yellowknives, the Tlicho, the Chipewyan, the Gwich'in, and the Slavey.

Historically, the Northern Athabaskans hunted and fished, depending on where they lived in different seasons. During the short summers, they fished and gathered edible plants. These included dandelions, moss, and nuts. They also gathered berries to dry. They

Many Native groups in the Subarctic have a ceremony known as a potlatch. During this ceremony, people gather for several days to eat, dance, and tell stories. In Northern Athabaskan culture, a potlatch is also a way for rich and powerful men to show their wealth. A potlatch typically occurs during a funeral or memorial for the dead. People often wear traditional caribou or moose hide and boots decorated with beads and rabbit fur.

mixed berries with meat and grease to create pemmican. This high-energy food helped them survive the long, cold winter. To make tools and utensils, they used stone, antlers, wood, and bone. They used birch bark and hides to make canoes.

Today, like other Arctic and Subarctic nations, the Northern Athabaskans mix traditional and modern living. They use dog sleds or snowmobiles to check traps. Many people wear jeans and other modern clothes. But these are often combined with traditional parkas, beaver-skin hats, and mittens.

Northern Athabaskans can be found in several Alaskan Native corporations in the United States and many First Nation governments in Canada. The Arctic Athabaskan Council (AAC) represents the rights and interests of American and Canadian Native Peoples. The AAC is involved in a variety of projects dealing with human rights. Other projects focus on environmental issues such as the relationship between Arctic peoples and the woodland caribou.

CHAPTER SIX

INNU

Innu boys hunt on the shores of Mistastin Lake in Labrador.

The Innu people, also known as the Naskapi, live in eastern Quebec and Labrador. They speak Innuaimun, a form of Cree. Traditionally, the Innu were nomadic hunters who followed the caribou. Much of their food came from this animal.

Innu children enjoy a ride on an all-terrain vehicle.

The Innu also used the caribou for clothing. Using the animal's skin, they made coats with elaborate designs. In addition, the Innu used the caribou's bones and antlers to make tools.

Historically, several families would live together in one lodge during winters. They used snowshoes, dog sleds, and toboggans for transportation. In summers, they would band together to socialize and trade. According to Innu culture, sadness causes weakness. For this reason, the Innu tend to joke and laugh even through bad times.

Today, about 16,000 Innu live in a dozen villages. Some live in remote areas. Many people make a living from logging and tourism.

In the late 1960s, the Canadian government flooded the Innu people's traditional lands to create a **hydroelectric** plant. In 2008, the Innu negotiated an agreement with the government of Newfoundland and Labrador. Known as the New Dawn Agreement, it included the Innu in a new hydroelectric project. The agreement was an attempt to pay them back for the flooding. It also gave them legal title to 5,000 square miles (13,000 sq km) of land, as well as hunting and fishing rights.

The Innu, like some other Native Peoples, practiced a spiritual ritual known as the Shaking Tent. The shaman would enter a tent, calling spiritual helpers with singing and drumming. These animal spirits would cry out and shake the tent. This would help cure the sick or ward off evil spells.

CHAPTER SEVEN

CREE

A group of Cree people cook food over a fire.

The Cree people occupy a larger area than any other Native group in Canada. They live in Quebec, Ontario, Manitoba, Saskatchewan, and Alberta. The name *Cree* comes from a mistake that French traders made when recording the tribal name

Cree hunters stand on a frozen lake in Manitoba.

Kenistenoag. The French wrote it as *Kristineaux* and later shortened it to *Cri*. In English, the name became known as Cree. In the Cree language, they are called the Nehiyawak.

In the 1600s, there were about 30,000 Cree. Today the population is more than 200,000, and there are many different groups of Cree spread over a wide area. Some of these groups, such as the Woodland Cree and the Swampy Cree, traditionally relied on hunting and fishing. They also gathered wild plants and berries. They used canoes, snowshoes, and toboggans to get around. In winters, they banded with relatives in family groups. During summers, they socialized in larger groups.

The Cree nations traded with European settlers during the fur trade era, which lasted from the early 1600s to the mid-1800s. This trading led some Cree groups to move west, where they quickly adapted to the use of horses and guns to hunt bison. But by the end of the 1800s, many Cree groups saw

Winter is the best time to see the aurora borealis.

their way of life dramatically changed. This was caused by several factors, including disease, the overhunting of bison, and government treaties requiring the Cree to live on reservations.

For more than 100 years, the Canadian government funded "residential schools," which were run by Christian religious groups. Native children throughout Canada, including many Cree, were separated from their families and communities. They were taken to live at the schools, where many students suffered abuse. Children were forced to speak English. They were punished for

One of the most beautiful natural phenomena in Earth's polar regions is the **aurora borealis**, or northern lights. These are dancing lights in the sky that form many shapes. Some look like curtains of light, while others look like arcs and streamers. They can be red, yellow, green, blue, or violet, but pink and green are the most common colors. Many Native Nations have oral traditions involving the northern lights. The Inuit call them *arsaniit* and say the lights are sky people playing ball games. The Cree say they are the dancing spirits of the dead. Some oral traditions say the lights are ancestors dancing to celebrate life. Others suggest that they come to collect recently departed souls.

speaking their own languages or following traditional cultural practices. As a result, much of the Cree culture was lost. A 2007 agreement gave an average of $20,000 each to about 110,000 Native Peoples who were affected by the schools. The agreement also included a public apology by Canada's prime minister.

In 1975, the Cree and Inuit peoples signed an agreement with the Canadian government. Known as the James Bay and Northern Quebec Agreement, it gave Native Nations more control over land rights and local government. Cree politicians have also played a large role in the Assembly of First Nations. This is the political organization representing Canada's 600 First Nations in their work toward self-government.

CHAPTER EIGHT

OJIBWE

An Ojibwe woman and daughter wear traditional dresses.

The Ojibwe, also known as the Chippewa, are one of the largest Native groups in North America. The name means "original people," and their language is a form of Algonquian. It is spoken by approximately 90,000 people today.

An Ojibwe basket contains pieces of leather and a type of shoes called moccasins.

Before European settlers arrived, the Ojibwe shared areas of Northern Ontario with the Cree. In the 1600s, the Ojibwe moved west and north because of the fur trade. Historically, the Ojibwe lived in small, independent bands that shared common traditions. Each band had a chief and specific hunting grounds. They formed villages for the summer and split into family groups for winter hunting.

When the Ojibwe moved into Northern Ontario and Manitoba, they blended with Cree communities. They relied on fishing and hunting. In particular, they used deer and moose for clothing and food. They traveled in birchbark canoes and lived in cone-shaped

The Ojibwe, along with the Cree and several other Native Nations, celebrate a tradition known as the powwow. Traditions, culture, art, and dance are featured in recreational and competitive events. During the grass dance, dancers imitate grass swaying in the wind. This is one of the oldest powwow dances. Dancers may also take part in the hoop dance. This is a form of storytelling in which the dancer forms shapes with hoops. These shapes may include butterflies, eagles, and snakes. Powwows may continue for a few hours or a few days, bringing people together to celebrate the nation's history and art.

wigwams. Men hunted or fished, while women tanned hides and made clothing. They gathered together in large groups to socialize and harvest maple syrup and wild rice.

Today, the Ojibwe have more than 160,000 members in Canada. They are one of the largest Native Nations in the United States. The Ojibwe are spread across five U.S. states and three Canadian provinces. Their leaders work toward economic and political independence.

There has been a resurgence of interest in the Ojibwe language. The Ojibwe people refer to their language as *Anishinaabe*. Some colleges and universities offer Ojibwe language classes. There are also tribal newspapers, language texts, and online resources such as the Ojibwe People's Dictionary.

SAY IT		
baby	biibii	(bee-bee)
canoe	jiimaan	(jee-man)
hello	boozhoo	(boo-joo)
thank you	miigwech	(mee-gwich)
bald eagle	migizi	(mi-gi-si)

CHAPTER NINE

ATIKAMEKW

The Atikamekw Nation lives in Quebec's Saint-Maurice River region. They are related to the Cree. From the late 1600s until the late 1900s, they were known as Têtes-de-Boules, which is French for "Round Heads."

Members of the Atikamekw Nation get ready to perform a traditional dance.

36

The Atikamekw were originally nomadic hunters. In the mid-1600s, tribal wars and European diseases took a heavy toll on the Atikamekw. By 1850, there were only about 150 Atikamekw left. Today, there are several thousand Atikamekw living in Canada.

Traditionally, their lives were based on hunting, fishing, trapping, and berry picking. Families lived in wigwams. Small family groups would band together for hunting in the winters and follow an experienced leader.

The Atikamekw share the legendary hero Wisakedjak with other Native groups such as the Cree and Ojibwe. This character tries to help people learn something, often by playing tricks on people or animals and being tricked in return. For the Atikamekw, though, he is usually portrayed as a friend.

In the early 1900s, rivers became home to mills and chemical industries. Hydroelectric energy and logging also became more common. This created environmental and social problems for the Atikamekw. Their water supply was even contaminated by the chemical mercury.

In 1972, the Atikamekw took back their original name, which means "Whitefish." In 1975, they formed a coalition with the Innu to help regain control over their lands. However, Canadian logging companies continued to use Atikamekw land. In 2014, the Atikamekw declared sovereignty over 30,000 square miles (80,000 sq km) of land and said they expect to be consulted on developments in the area. They continue their effort to exert control over their ancestral rights in the area.

aboriginal (AB-uh-RIJ-uh-nul) Aboriginal means native to a certain place. Aboriginal people were the first humans to live in North America.

aurora borealis (ah-ROR-ah bor-ee-AH-lis) The aurora borealis, also called the northern lights, are bands of light appearing in the sky at night. The aurora borealis come in many colors, but pink and green are the most common.

harpoons (har-POONZ) Harpoons are spears used to hunt animals that live underwater. The Inuit hunt seals with harpoons.

hides (HYDZ) Hides are the skins of animals with the flesh scraped off. Caribou hides are used for parkas and pants.

hydroelectric (HY-dro-ee-LEK-trik) Hydroelectric means having to do with the use of moving water to create electricity. Dams provide hydroelectric energy.

kayaks (KY-aks) Kayaks are small, lightweight boats with covered tops and holes for people to sit inside. People fit snugly inside kayaks, so water does not get into the boats.

migrations (my-GRAY-shunz) Migrations happen when animals move away from one place to live in another place. Many bird migrations cover thousands of miles.

nomadic (no-MAD-ic) Nomadic means moving from place to place and not settling down. Nomadic peoples do not build permanent cities.

self-determination (SELF di-tur-muh-NAY-shun) Self-determination is a group's freedom to choose its own government. In the past, European settlers often made the laws, but today many Native Nations are seeking self-determination.

shamans (SHAH-manz) Shamans are people who are thought to have special spiritual powers. Shamans lead ceremonies that are intended to help people heal.

tundra (TUHN-dra) Tundra is a level, treeless plain in the Arctic. The tundra is frozen for much of the year.

TO LEARN MORE

BOOKS

Cunningham, Kevin and Peter Benoit. *The Inuit.* New York: Children's Press, 2011.

Dwyer, Helen, and Mary Stout. *Cree History and Culture.* New York: Gareth Stevens, 2012.

Peoples of the Arctic and Subarctic. Chicago: World Book, 2009.

WEB SITES

Visit our Web site for links about Native Nations of the Arctic and Subarctic:

childsworld.com/links

Note to Parents, Teachers, and Librarians: We routinely verify our Web links to make sure they are safe and active sites. So encourage your readers to check them out!